Women on the Verge of HRT

A play

Marie Jones

Music by Neil Martin

Samuel French — London
New York - Toronto - Hollywood

WOMEN ON THE VERGE OF HRT

Women on the Verge of HRT premièred at The West
Belfast Festival Feile and Phobail in August, 1995 with
the following cast:

Vera	Marie Jones
Anna	Eileen Pollock
Fergal	Dan Gordon

Directed by Pam Brighton
Musical Direction/Keyboards — Brian O'Neill
Fiddle — Cathal Hayden

Subsequently presented by Jenny King and Pat Moylan
for Centreline Productions (UK) and Dubbeljoint Media
at the Vaudeville Theatre, London on 19th February,
1997 with the following cast:

Vera	Marie Jones
Anna	Eileen Pollock
Fergal	Dessie Gallagher

Directed by Pam Brighton
Designed by Robert Ballagh
Lighting by Eileen O'Reilly
Original Music by Neil Martin

Musical Director/Keyboards — Brian O'Neill
Fiddle — Cathal Hayden

CHARACTERS

Vera
Anna
Fergal

The action takes place in a bedroom in Daniel O'Donnell's hotel - *The Viking House Hotel* - in Kincasslagh and on the beach of Donegal bay

Time — the present

ACKNOWLEDGEMENTS

The White Birds by W. B. Yeats is included with the kind permission of A. P. Watt Ltd on behalf of Michael B. Yeats.

MUSICAL NUMBERS

ACT I

ACT II

Please note that the musical material for these numbers is to be found on p.45. An enlarged version of the music is available on free loan from Samuel French Ltd.

A licence issued by Samuel French Ltd to perform this play only includes permission to use the songs by Neil Martin specified in this copy. If any other music is used in conjuction with this play permission must be sought as under:

Where the place of performance is already licensed by the PERFORMING RIGHT SOCIETY a return of the music used must be made to them. If the place of performance is not so licensed then application should be made to the Performing Right Society, 29 Berners Street, London W1.

A separate and additional licence from PHONOGRAPHIC PERFORMANCES LTD, 1 Upper James Street, London W1R 3HG is needed whenever commercial recordings are used.

In the original production of *Women on the Verge of HRT* the play opened with a short film, "The Daniel O'Donnell Weekend", footage of women queuing to meet Daniel O'Donnell at one of his famous tea parties in Kincasslagh in Donegal. This takes place every summer when thousands of women travel from as far away as America and New Zealand to meet Daniel in person.

ACT I

A room in The Viking House Hotel (*owned by Daniel O'Donnell*)

There are two beds, a dressing-table, bedside cabinets and a door SR *into the bathroom. The main door* SL, *leads to the hotel corridor. On one cabinet is a telephone*

Music: I Want to Dance With You *by Daniel O'Donnell*

The House Lights and music fade

The Lights come up

Anna's and Vera's bags are in the room. Vera's rather large toilet bag and towel are on her bed. Anna's spectacles and a huge romantic novel are placed on her bedside cabinet

Anna is in her nightie preparing for bed. She is humming I Want to Dance With You. *She brings a pillowcase out of her bag and quickly puts it on the pillow on her bed. She lifts it up and starts to smooth it out gently. We see that it is a pillowcase with a picture of Daniel on it. She then places it on her bed. She brings out her soap bag and takes out a tub of Nivea Creme. She looks across to the other bed and looks enviously at Vera's toilet bag. She goes over to the door and listens while still watching the bag. She then rushes over and looks inside the bag — she produces a large tub of expensive cream*

Anna (*checking the bottom of the jar*) Jesus Christ. Twenty-seven quid. (*She opens the jar and takes a large dollop and smoothes it over her face*) Oh God you can't half tell the difference. (*She smoothes the cream over to cover up the dent in it and puts the lid back on and carefully replaces it in Vera's bag. She lifts the pillow and starts to sway with it, singing*)

She gets into bed and places the pillow carefully beside her in the bed. She puts on her glasses and opens her novel and starts to read — a perfect end to a perfect day

Vera enters

Vera Bastard. (*To Anna*) Dessie McClure is a rotten stinkin' bastard.

Vera storms into the bathroom

Anna Oh no. Here we go again.

Vera comes out of the bathroom and lifts her towel

Vera I can just see his oul pasty gub. Bastard.
Anna Sure you can't stand him.
Vera You're right. I can't stand him. He can't stand me; that's fair. He hit me. I hit him back harder. Also fair. But this is not fair. Bastard.

Vera goes back into the bathroom

Anna You were great all day. Never mentioned nothing. You were carried away with Daniel like the rest of us. (*Shouting into the bathroom*) I thought you got over it.
Vera (*off*) I've been on the vodka down at the bar, and you know me on vodka.
Anna Think too much for your own good.
Vera I hope it gurns all night and keeps the oul pig up.
Anna Ack now that's not fair on that wee child.

Vera comes out of the bathroom in a very flash dressing-gown and revealing nightdress

Vera Fair? Don't talk to me about fair! I can just hear him now. "My son. My son and heir." Heir to what? His frigging dole cheque.

Vera throws the towel down on the floor then proceeds to take off her make-up and put on her night creams

Anna Vera, get a grip, he married somebody twenty-five years younger. It was only a matter of time.
Vera He's fifty! He is fifty and he'll be waltzin' round Crazy Prices with his new buggy and bummin' and blowin' and doing the proud father bit. Big slabber. Little does his wee wifey know it'll be her wheeling him round Crazy Prices in another couple of years.
Anna Surely to God you're not jealous.
Vera It has nothin' to do with being jealous. Her and the child are welcome to him. It's just — it's just that it doesn't happen the other way round, does it?

Anna What? Sure you wouldn't want kids at your age.

Vera What if I did.

Anna But I know you don't and you know you don't, so what is the problem?

Vera The problem is that bastard can and it is not fair. I said to him after our last one, "Right, you are for the snip." Jesus! You'd have thought I was asking him to go and get it amputated. "Oh no. Oh no," says he. "Sure I wouldn't feel like a real man." — a real man? And all the time the bastard was making sure he kept his options open so that someday he could live out his fantasy of a young one on his arm. Pig.

Anna Vera, I have read the same bit six times.

Vera Sorry.

Anna Oh God, I can't believe that we're here in Donegal. Daniel was brilliant, wasn't he?

Vera Aye, Anna I'm sorry. I need to get this out of me or I'll go mental. It is the thought of him getting one up on me that I can't have.

Anna He didn't do it to get at you.

Vera Oh did he not, did he not? I remember one night him coming home from the club like a baitin' bear, wouldn't say what was wrong with him. So anyway the next day I see one of his mates and I says, "Here. What was up with Dessie last night? He came home ready to kill dead things." Well, apparently some fella called him cissy prick.

Anna Why?

Vera Because he only has daughters and it near killed him. Oh aye, thought he wasn't a real man 'cos he didn't have his man child to carry on the line. What fucking line! The only line he knows is the one he stands in to sign on.

Anna Aye, but it does go deep with some men.

Vera Deep! Deep! See if we lived in one of them Muslim countries he would be quite happy to lock me and our girls up in the back yard and put black veils on us.

There is a knock at the door

Anna Who's that?

Vera I ordered drinks.

Anna Ah for God sake. Look at the time.

Fergal enters, carrying a tray with two glasses of vodka

Vera continues with her creams etc. ignoring him. She stops to bend down to pick up the towel. Fergal is behind her and almost bumps into her — she continues and ignores him

Fergal places the two glasses on Anna's bedside cabinet

Vera Of course when I pointed it out to him that it was the man that determined the sex he was all agog.

Anna (*getting her purse*) Much is that love?

Vera Put it on our bill.

Anna No. I'd rather pay now.

Vera "How come?" This is what he actually says to me. "How come", he says, "it's my fault?"

Fergal Four eighty, please.

Vera "Fault? Are you calling my three daughters a fault?"

Anna (*giving Fergal the money*) Thanks, love.

Fergal No problem. (*He watches Vera*)

Vera I says, "You are one stupid bastard."

Fergal has been watching Vera and listening. He turns to walk away, still watching her, and trips and falls over the bed. Vera stops momentarily, then carries on

"There is a male and a female sperm."

Fergal (*staring at them both; embarrassed*) I didn't know that.

Fergal exits

Anna Vera. That fella was all cut — you talking about sperm in front of him.

Vera Well he shouldn't have been frigging listening. (*She goes to her bag and takes out her vitamin pills, washing them down with the vodka*) I says, "Dessie, do you want me to draw you a wee diagram?" So I actually had to draw it for him. Course, that made it worse when he realized it was his fault. Oh, if it was my fault he could handle it, but not him.

Anna I didn't want a drink — I'm just nice. I've had just enough. Oh Vera! I near died when Daniel said that. To think that he remembered our names and it was months ago when we told him. "Hello Anna, nice to see you. Hello Vera. How are you doing? Nice to see you both." Did you not near die, I did.

Vera is not listening to Anna, she is carried away with her own thoughts. She throws off her dressing-gown and slumps on the bed

Vera Like what did she see in him? Know what I mean. He has nothing. Never had nothing. He has no money, no hobbies, no interests and she is twenty-five years younger.

Anna (*annoyed*) She may have seen something you didn't.

Vera It's not bloody fair.

Anna For Christ sake, you wouldn't take a gift of him.

Vera Yes, but I would take the gift of somebody. He has Susie and I am on
my own — probably always will be. It's the thought of the rest of my life
on my own. I don't even like my own company. I am better with people.

Anna You have plenty of friends.

Vera Don't you start pensioning me off now.

Anna What did I say?

Vera You could have said, "Ack, Vera, sure you're not that old. Sure maybe
you'll meet somebody." But plenty of friends? Did any of Dessie's mates
say that to him when we split up? " Dessie; sure you have your friends."
They did me arse. More like. "Here Dessie. You got rid of Vera. You can
welt away till your nose bleeds." But not me. Sure I have friends. Thanks
a lot, Anna.

Anna Well I am just being realistic, Vera. Just in case it never happens you
have to prepare yourself.

Vera Fuck! I love that. Prepare myself. How do you prepare for being on the
sexual scrap heap? Do we all book into a sex hospice? Is there a class you
can go to? Like a lie-down-and-die class? Do all us over-forties bring our
sexy underwear and our face creams and throw them on a big bonfire —
and some oul doll in a kimono makes us beat up a big plastic willy. Come
on now, ladies — drive out those evil thoughts. Banish that nasty libido.
Rid from your memory that horrible penis.

Anna Oh God, she would only have to say that word and she would put me
off. I hate that word.

Vera It's all right for you, Anna, you have your Marty. You're all right. You
don't understand.

Anna I do understand, Vera. I just think you are getting too carried away.
Anyway since you and Dessie split up you've only ever stayed with a fella
for a matter of months. Always choppin' and changin'. I don't know why
you couldn't make do.

Vera I wanted to shop around. Where's the harm in that? The harm is the
shop is about to shut and I haven't done my messages yet. Anna, it's like
going for your groceries at a quarter past five and you hear this voice, "This
store will be closing in fifteen minutes." And what do you do? You panic
and you grab something you don't want. That's what I am scared of. Panic
buying.

Song No. 1: I Won't Go Easy

(*Singing*)	I don't want to be on my own.
	I won't give up tryin' to score.
Anna	She never wanted the one she had
	And now she wants one more.

Vera	A lonely bed is a desolate place
	Like a sky without a star.
Anna	She couldn't wait to be rid of him
	To get runnin' off to the bar.

Vera I won't go easy, I'll go down protestin'
The rest of my life is too long for restin'
All I'm askin' is the right to reply
When I'm told my passion must lie down and die.

It's not that I want a man
I just want to know that I can if I want.

Anna When she had one she didn't at all
Now she hasn't she wants them all.

Vera Lonely nights are drawing near
Like a darkness that goes on forever.

Anna The day he left, she vowed
Men and her, never, never, never.

Vera I won't go easy, I'll go down protestin'
The rest of my life is too long for restin'
All I'm askin' is the right to reply
When I'm told my passion must lie down and die.

Anna Why don't you get a cat?

Vera Are you tying to be fuckin' funny? (*She lifts the phone*)

Anna You should get to sleep.

Vera Hello reception. Two vodkas and two white lemonades, please. Room eleven. (*To Anna*) I am not tired. I'm too pissed off.

Vera goes into the bathroom

Anna No I was serious, I was reading an article and they say the reason why an awful lot of middle-aged women get cats is because, well, like they have all this love and because it is not that easy for middle-aged women to meet men they can sort of put all the love into the cats — you know somewhere for it to go.

Vera comes out with a lit cigarette

Anna sees the cigarette; Vera has broken her promise about smoking in the room

Vera, you promised.

Vera (*ignoring Anna; waving the smoke away*) Could you see me going for a smelly oul cat instead of a good screw?

Anna You don't understand. It's a way of getting rid of them sort of feelings — you sort of put it into the cat.

Vera The day you look in my window and see me lookin' out and stroking a cat and wondering what I'm going to make it for its tea, shoot me. Remember Mary out of work that breeds the wee terriers? What do we all say about her, "Ack God love her it's her wee substitute babies." Just because she's over forty and not married. Mary told me she doesn't like kids. She prefers dogs. But would anybody listen? No, she's only protestin' because she can't handle not having kids. But then who would listen to the likes of us — just a big mass of middle-aged nobodies.

Anna Now don't talk rubbish.

Vera I am right. Do you see when you don't interest men with the possibility of sex? They can't be bothered to get to know you. Like, what is the point in putting in the effort? Far too boring.

Anna Sex isn't everything, Vera.

Vera Yes it is and don't let anybody tell you any different.

Anna It doesn't bother me.

Vera That's because you have a man.

Anna It's not. Plenty of women with men that can't be bothered.

Vera Aye and plenty have no choice. Why do you read all them stupid oul romantic books if you're not interested?

Anna I like a good love story.

Vera Yes and so do I. But my own. Not somebody else's. We are supposed to just be content with somebody else's excitement. Well fuck that for a game of darts.

Anna This has all just happened 'cos of your Dessie, you were happy enough until that wee child came.

Vera I wasn't happy. I pretended I was. Anna, the last time I went out with somebody was well over a year.

Anna Oh aye, I liked him.

Vera He was all right.

Anna He wanted to marry you.

Vera So? I didn't want to marry him. Oh I know that's what everybody thought. "Oh Vera this could be your last chance, don't knock it." They even had me thinking like that. Then I caught myself on. You know what really gets me, Anna, I am starting to get embarrassed to talk about sex and men and stuff — you know in case people start to laugh at me.

Anna Nobody would laugh.

Vera I don't mean laugh. More thinking I am ridiculous — pathetic — and then that bastard and his wee bride and his wee baby and all the lads clapping him on the back. "Oh well done there, Dessie. I see the oul weapon

is still in good working order. See you haven't run out of ammunition yet."
Christ! It makes me so sick. (*She throws herself on to the bed in frustration*)
Anna Vera, you are going to have to come to terms with all this. I mean not
just your Dessie and the child.

There is a knock at the door

Cover yourself up.

Anna throws Vera's dressing-gown over Vera and goes to open the door

Vera (*throwing the dressing-gown off on to the floor*) I am covered up.
Anna You know what I mean.
Vera This cost me an arm and a leg and I'm covering it up for nobody.

*Fergal comes in with two vodkas trying desperately to avert his eyes from
Vera who is sprawled on the bed in her nightie*

Anna I'll just get the money. (*She pays for the drinks*) Thanks.
Fergal No problem.

Fergal smiles. Anna turns away and Fergal has a sneak look at Vera

Fergal leaves

Anna He was nice.
Vera I never took much notice.
Anna He noticed you, Vera McClure.
Vera Did he?
Anna Aye. Well, I mean he noticed the nightie.
Vera I should think so.
Anna He forgot the mixers, I'll get him up again.
Vera What for?
Anna He's forgotten the mixers. We could get him back up again and have
a wee yarn with him.
Vera And what would he find to talk to us about?
Anna We're not that stupid.
Vera I don't like younger men anymore. I get bored with young ones. I want
to talk to somebody. You know. Have a conversation. I actually like
talking.
Anna I know what you mean.

Vera sings to herself a parody of Daniel's song — I Want to Dance With You.
Vera repeats, the song, becoming more frustrated. Suddenly she jumps up
singing it in full voice whilst dancing wildly about the room. Anna joins in —
getting giddy and excited. Vera suddenly stops

I think I'm cracking up.
Anna I'm gonna get him up. (*She lifts the phone*)
Vera No!
Anna Yes!
Vera Wait till I put my make-up on.

Vera goes to her case and hurriedly brings out her make-up bag then jumps
back on the bed

Anna (*lifting the phone*) Hello reception. Could we have two white
lemonades please— room eleven, thanks.

Vera reapplies her make-up

Vera Oh God, Anna. Is this desperation stages?
Anna No, it's more "Why not?" stages. Or "If you're not in you can't win"
stages.
Vera We're not as bad as that woman who wants to buy Daniel's underpants,
are we?
Anna Wise up, you don't want Daniel's underpants, do you?
Vera No — but is it the same desperation — desperate to have something
that you know you can't have.
Anna Sure. Weren't we like that when we were sixteen. I remember going
to *Romano's* on a Saturday night and if you didn't get off with somebody
you were suicidal because you had a whole week to wait and that was a
lifetime when you were sixteen. I remember going in at nine o'clock you
were dead picky because you knew you had three hours left. Only Elvis
look-alikes would suffice. By ten o'clock your standards had started to
drop a wee bit and you would accept the odd harelip or dodgy eye. By
eleven o'clock you could feel the panic comin' on and you had to rethink
the ones you snubbed earlier but they had been snapped up by the less picky
and by five to twelve all they were required to do was walk, talk and
breathe.
Vera Still deep down you knew you had endless Saturday nights to come.

There is a knock at the door

Anna Vera I will go into the bathroom and let on I'm taking a bath or
something and you talk to him, OK. (*She moves to open the door*)

*Vera is not sure if this is a good idea, but it's too late to argue, she dashes to
her case to conceal her make-up bag. As she turns, Anna is about to let Fergal
in the door. Vera hurriedly jumps back on the bed — she can't get to her own
in time so she sits on Anna's trying to appear casual and in control*

> *Anna moves into the rooom with Fergal behind her. He is carrying two
> unopened bottles of lemonade — Anna takes the towel and heads for the
> bathroom*

Excuse me.

Anna exits into the bathroom

Fergal stands with the bottles of lemonade

Fergal Mixers? Sorry about that.
Vera Thanks.

*She nods towards the bedside table for Fergal to set them. He does so and is
about to leave*

You haven't got an opener, have you?

*Fergal produces a bottle opener, opens the bottles and "disappears" the
bottle opener*

That was a brilliant trick.
Fergal That wasn't a trick. That was magic.

He is about to leave when Vera stops him

Vera What's your name?
Fergal Fergal.
Vera You live in Donegal then?
Fergal Aye, just down the road. Are you enjoying yourself then? I tell you,
youse women mustn't get away often. I am run off my feet the night. The
roars and laughs coming from them rooms. Parties going on all over the
place. I love these nights. The women that come down from the North are
great crack. You know I was meant to be off and I asked Kathleen could
I work. I don't mind staying up all night — you get a great laugh. There is
about ten of them down the corridor and they are having a ball. They keep
ordering coke and lemonade but every time I go they seem to be drunker.

Vera Must be the air. Would you like a drink?

Fergal (*hesitates for a second as if he shouldn't*) Aye, don't mind if I do. (*He notices the pillow*) He's great, isn't he? (*Pause*) Daniel is great isn't he?

Vera (*quickly*) This isn't my bed.

Fergal He definitely brings out the best in people. Are you from the North yourself then?

Vera Aye, Belfast. Me and my friend always ——

Fergal I couldn't live in the city. I went to New York a couple of years back to get work. Dreamt about Donegal every night. I couldn't wait to get home. Especially nights like this. When I finish I'll go away off to the headland there and just sit and watch the dawn comin' in. Nowhere like it in the world. You can just lose yourself in the sheer beauty of it. Magic it is. For all New York has to offer you can't beat Donegal on a summer morning. There was six boys and four girls in our family and everyone of us are still here, isn't that some going? Sure working in this place you get to meet people from everywhere, I mean why leave a place like this when you can meet the world here in Kincasslagh — I thought about getting a few animals but there is no money in it so I do a bit of this and a bit of that, and thank God for Daniel and I get by — where's your friend?

Vera Having a bath — well me and her …

Fergal I was born here and I'll die here. Not very ambitious but I'm content. Know what I mean? And that means a lot, you know, to be at peace with yourself. The day I wake up in a morning and look out my bedroom window and not see the beauty of this place is the day I'll have to go — know what I mean? If this place becomes like anywhere in the world then I might as well be anywhere in the world, but thank God it hasn't happened yet. I wrote a song about here when I was in New York — I'm going to sing it for you. (*He sings in the style of Daniel O'Donnell*)

Song No. 2: Donegal

I dream of the dawn in the land of my birth
My soul hears its silent call
To the magic and glory of that wonderous sight
Of the dawn over Donegal.

On still summer nights my heart is torn
As I stand on this foreign shore
Oh Donegal at each rising dawn
I will yearn for you ever more.

Instrumental verse whilst Fergal talks to Vera

Fergal (*Daniel-like*) Well hello there and what's your name?

Vera Wise up.

Fergal Ack now don't be shy what's your name?

Vera (*laughing*) Vera.

Fergal Ack God isn't that a beautiful name — and Vera are you here by yourself or are you with a friend?

Vera (*now playing along*) No, I'm here with my friend.

Fergal Well Vera this is for you and your friend.

> (*Singing*) This foreign land cannot erase
> Those pictures so clear in my mind
> Where the setting sun brings peace to my soul
> Oh my dear land I've left behind.

He sits on the bed and sings to her

> Should I die on this alien shore
> I pray that my soul will away
> Across the seas to my heaven on earth
> Donegal, where my spirit will stay.

Well ladies and gentlemen, I feel at this point I haft to come among you.

Instrumental, two verses. Fergal goes into the audience and talks to them just like Daniel. Fergal comes back on stage

> I dream of the dawn in the land of my birth
> My soul hears its silent call
> To the magic and glory of that wonderous sight
> Of the dawn over Donegal.

He finishes the song and then sits on the bed and smiles at Vera

(*Speaking*) Sure, we can't all be Daniel.

Vera Are you married?

Fergal What? No fear, too much responsibility, sure plenty of time yet.

Vera (*disheartened*) Well, Fergal, you certainly have it all sorted out.

Fergal For now anyway and sure that's all as far as anybody can get, you know what I mean? — Like you can't get ahead of yourself 'cos you don't know what is ahead and I think if you look too far forward you stop enjoying now because you are too concerned with up ahead. God. You women will keep me talking all night and I have work to do. No doubt I'll see yis later — if I come out of that party down the corridor alive.

Fergal leaves

Anna enters from the bathroom

Anna Well?

Vera There is talking and there is talking, but somebody has injected that fella with something.

Anna Did you flirt with him? Give him the eye?

Vera Give him the eye? If I had taken it out of its socket and handed it to him I don't think he would have noticed.

Anna Still he had something to talk about; you know what I mean? All that about the beauty of this place. When you have all this around you it does help you to see into yourself — be more interesting. Maybe that's why Daniel is so genuine — it kind of humbles you, all this nature stuff.

Vera What are you talking about?

Anna Well I suppose when you are surrounded by the beauty of nature all the time, it does you. Like what I mean is, maybe you don't need to go luking for an ornament to put on your arm — you know the way some men do.

Vera Anna, we don't live in Donegal. We live in Belfast and whether you like it or not we have passed our sell-by date.

Anna There is no talking to you, is there?

Vera I'm sorry, Anna, sorry for laying all this on you. It was just him and the baby upset me. I'll just lie down and forget about it. Yes, Vera it's time to buy the crimplene frocks and content yourself.

Anna Ack, Vera. I couldn't see you like that.

Vera Anna. I stood in the changing room of C &A the other day with a whole pile of clothes and I didn't know what to buy. I just stood there looking in the mirror and I says; Vera, you don't know what you are supposed to look like anymore. How do other people see you? For a moment I wished I lived in one of them African tribes where they don't wear any clothes from they're born till they die.

Anna Vera. For God sake, it's not that bad.

Vera It's all right for you. You have Marty. You're happy. Just leave me to come to terms with this myself.

Anna You're a laugh. You come in here. You put me off my book, depress me about things and then you just go to sleep.

Vera I said I'm sorry.

Anna Why don't we see if we can join that party down the corridor.

Vera What! They are all about sixty.

Anna Doesn't mean they are not having a good time.

Vera Jesus listen to me, Anna. I see all them mins and I see the future looking at me in the face and I can't bear it.

Anna They are having a good time.

Vera Because they have just seen Daniel. He loves them and that makes them feel good, feel important. He remembers their names and wee things about them and he enjoys them — but that is it — that is it. I don't want to be content with that. They love him because he treats them like real people — important enough to remember but how do other people treat them?

Anna I don't know what you are on about.

Vera (*imitating a male voice*) All right sexy — what about you duchess, enjoying your wee drink? Now too much of that gets a girl pregnant.

Anna Aye, but that is only good fun.

Vera I mean nobody can deal with old women and sex seriously. That's what we are on the verge of, Anna.

Anna I never think about it.

Vera You see all these big stars in America that were once really beautiful and sexy and now they spend thousands trying to stay that way just so they won't get ignored — not get taken seriously. Whoever said beauty is in the eye of the beholder is a lying bastard. It is in the hands of them that are making a bloody fortune.

Anna Well, Vera, there is no way you could afford one of them face jobs.

Vera See if I could, I bloody would.

Anna Ack no, then you wouldn't be you, Vera.

Vera Why, who would I be?

Anna I mean you can't disguise them face jobs. People would say, there is Vera McClure and we all know what age Vera is and yet there is Vera with a face of a woman of thirty. She must be desperate for a man.

Vera (*sudden burst of anger*) I am not desperate for a man. It's fear. Fear of not being heard — becoming invisible. If only I had the money — I don't care — I would buy it: I could actually buy me another ten years. Maybe more, depending on the plastic surgeon. I would have the best.

Anna Clint Eastwood's face in *The Bridges of Madison County* is a mass of wrinkles and he was voted the sexiest man in Hollywood. And him that has enough money to change his whole body if he tuk the notion but he doesn't have to because the weemin love him the way he is — now that's not fair.

Vera I rest my case. And you know what is worse? There is sweet f. a. you can do about it.

Anna I know like there is nothing.

Vera Nothin' …

Anna Nothin' at all.

Vera Zilch.

Anna This is depressing.

Vera Tell me about it.

Anna Dead depressing.

Vera I know.

Anna So there's nothing you can do about it?
Vera No.
Anna So like I say Vera, you put up and shut up.
Vera No! You put up, but you don't shut up.

Vera goes into bathroom

Anna Mouthing on about it won't change it. Most women accept that they
   get old.
Vera (*from the bathroom*)I am not going to go quietly.
Anna You're not going anywhere.

Vera comes out of the bathroom with a lit cigarette

Vera Anna. You have just accepted that you are not sexy anymore. You have
   accepted that when you walk into a room nobody will notice you. Anna?
   Anna who? You have just accepted you are invisible.
Anna Vera, you should go and see the doctor. You are getting too carried
   away with all this. You're getting too deep for your own good.
Vera Go to the doctor and get what?
Anna I think you are going through the change.
Vera (*screaming in frustration*) I KNEW YOU WERE GOING TO SAY
   THAT. That's just the answer I would have expected. So I am talking shite.
   None of what I am saying is comin' out of the mouth of a sane woman
   because she is on the verge of the change of life. So I go to the doctor and
   I can see him now. Not even looking at me. Just shrugging his shoulders
   and saying, "Well Vera, you know it could be the menopause." No! That's
   too easy, that's what I am supposed to believe to explain why I am in this
   state. Well they won't get me on that one, no way.
Anna You can get something, you know, to make you feel better if it is the
   change, not that I am saying it is, but if it was.
Vera Get something? Like what.
Anna I don't know.
Vera What did you get?
Anna Nothing.
Vera And why should I get something.
Anna Well when I heard that, that HRT makes you, you know, want sex I
   just says — Doctor, keep it.
Vera Why?
Anna Nothing — just — I says keep it.
Vera Keep it?
Anna Yes — I'm going to sleep — give it a rest, Vera.
Vera Hold on. Hold on. Now it's different for me. What would be the point

of me getting something that makes me want to have sex when I haven't got anybody to have sex with. I would say, "Doctor that is torture", but you that has a man are saying keep it?

Anna I'm sorry I brought it up, why do you have to go into everything. You can't leave nothing alone, everything always has to be gone into — picked over — never leave well enough alone, you.

Vera Jesus, don't ate my head off.

Anna Go to sleep will you.

Vera OK. OK. I said I'm sorry.

Anna And I'm fed up with you saying, "You're all right, you've got Marty". I don't see why you think anybody with a man is all right when you couldn't hack any of the ones you got. I mean, like, are you the only woman in Belfast that has a bad deal? Well you're not. It's just the rest of us don't go on and on like a broken record about it.

Vera I said I'm sorry, good-night.

Anna (*lying down and then getting up again*) No. You have a right cheek. You get me started and then you just say you're going to sleep. Well let me tell you something. Don't ever let me hear you saying, "You're all right, you have got Marty." Because do you see if it wasn't for Daniel and his music I would go mental — bloody crazy — that fella keeps me going.

Vera (*shocked*) Jesus, Anna.

Anna I know he doesn't know me or anything but he lifts me. The songs lift me. Marty laughs. "What would a fella like that see in a crowd of ould dolls. Think Daniel O'Donnell would look twice at you?" But I just bite my lip and say nothing but you know what I want to say? I want to say, "Marty he makes me feel good, he lets me imagine, lets me escape from the boredom of having to live with you." You know our ones bought us a weekend away in London for our twenty-fifth wedding anniversary and I couldn't handle it. I thought how in God's name am I going to get through a whole weekend with him on my own? What under God are we going to talk about? So the day before I let on I was sick. I says Marty we will have to cancel this because I am not one bit well and the look of relief on his face was a picture. He even brought me up a cup of tea to bed he was that delighted and I looked at him and I said to myself, "You know if he knew how to talk we wouldn't be married because to leave each other would mean having to have a serious conversation, and the idea of a serious conversation would put him in the hospital." I had a few drinks on me one night and I said, "Marty, why do you never make love to me anymore?" and he got up and walked out of the room and didn't speak for about a week. Too frightened in case I brought it up again. So I never. So that's that.

Vera (*livid*) Leave him. Leave him. Don't say nothing, just leave.

Anna (*aghast*) And be on my own?

Vera You might as well not be there anyway.

Anna Aye, right enough. You're a great advert for being on your own.

Vera At least I am not living with somebody who ignores me.

Anna He is there, isn't he? He still lives with me; hasn't left; probably never will.

Vera How do you know that?

Anna He couldn't cope on his own, he hasn't the maturity of a ten year old.

Vera Jesus Christ.

Anna There is worse marriages than mine—at least he doesn't interfere with what I do and that suits me.

Vera goes to her suitcase and takes out a bottle of vodka

Vera Emergency supplies.

There is an awkward pause after the row. They drink

Anna You see that waiter? He spoke to you like you were just equal — I would settle for that but if it is not to be then it is not to be.

Vera I never knew that about you and Marty.

Anna Don't you be telling anybody. I don't say, because who wants to know, there is nothing you can do.

There is a knock at the door

Vera Who is it?

Fergal Fergal.

Vera quickly conceals the vodka back into her suitcase then goes to let Fergal in

Fergal enters and sees Anna and Vera both in the dumps

Would you believe it? I have been instructed by room fourteen to get you girls down to the party. You might as well. Sure nobody sleeps the night.

Vera No thanks. We're tired.

Fergal Tired? Now don't give me that. Sure the place is hopping.

Anna It was a long oul day.

Fergal Wasn't Daniel brilliant? They just love him to bits. I swear to God he has that crowd down there dancing about like two year olds and half of them they tell me are getting the disability. If the Government man came into that room he could save the country a fortune. You'd swear they'd all been to Lourdes and all on mixers. I can't believe it.

Vera Surely to God you're not that gullible.

Anna Vera.

Fergal Sorry?

Vera Nothing.

Fergal Oh, you mean do I not know they have the contents of an off-licence in their suitcases? No. I don't know because I don't want to spoil it for them. (*He looks at Vera*) Sure if you don't fancy the party there's always the dawn.

Vera is confused — is this an offer?

Just giving you the message; it's up to you.

Fergal leaves

Anna What a nice bloke.

Vera Too nice.

Anna What's that supposed to mean?

Vera I don't know. He would remind you of him (*indicating Daniel on the pillowcase*) wouldn't he?

Anna God now when you think of it he would. He would.

Vera The same kind of way with him.

Anna Yes. Anyway, I am going. I need a laugh. Come on.

Vera No.

Anna (*getting out of bed*) Well I am not letting Marty Morrison get to me. If they spent as much time getting depressed over us as we did over them the world would be a far fairer place. Come on, Vera. We have looked forward to this night for a whole year — a whole year.

Vera You know I sat in the concert tonight and I watched all those women and they were ecstatic watching Daniel, and that made me really bloody sad.

Anna Sad? How could you? You love him.

Vera I love the music and the songs and I see me in the song and it's my love story. What happens when you don't see yourself in the song anymore? What happens? It's not fair. Dessie has Susie on his arm to make him feel young again and I can do nothing.

Anna Vera, will you stop. So it's not fair. I am away to this party, I am sorry, I know you're depressed; so am I many a time but I have had enough for one night. Now I am getting ready and I am going. I mean why aren't they all depressed down in room fourteen?

Vera Because they know it's over.

Anna Yes and so do I. Now I am going. Come on.

Anna goes into the bathroom

Vera tosses and turns on the bed in frustration

Anna re-enters wearing her dressing gown

Vera Don't leave me on my own.

Anna Then come on. It's the change. I told you.

Vera So what is supposed to happen to me — this change?

Anna Well, there's the flushes for a start. I used to flare up like a beetroot. God. Dead embarrassing in company. It used to drive Marty mad. And then he would whisper to whoever was in our company "It's the change". He wouldn't even say the word. He might as well as been saying leprosy the way he twisted his face and rolled his eyes. He just mimed it like I had some kind of terminal illness. No. Worse than that. Some kind of mental illness. Like he was telling other people I was a bit funny on it.

Vera And you let him away with it?

Anna Well I was sort of embarrassed too. I didn't want people to know.

Vera Why?

Anna Well it's not a thing you go round broadcasting.

Vera Why?

Anna I don't know, Vera. It just isn't.

Vera Well I'm not going to go quietly.

Anna You'll get over it.

Vera I wish I had them all lined up so I could tell them exactly what they are doing to us.

Anna Who, for Christ sake?

Vera I don't know — Dessie. His mates. All the ones that treat us like we are stupid ignorant cows. Your Marty.

Anna You will say nothing to my Marty. Oh God, I hate telling you anything.

Vera All right then I'll leave your Marty out of it, but I would love to line up the rest.

Anna And then what?

Vera Then I will have satisfaction.

Anna You definitely need help, Vera. (*She goes to the door*) You know where I am.

Vera (*as Anna goes*) Oh no, Anna, you are the one that needs help.

Anna exits

Song No. 3: I Want to Be

(*singing*)   I want to be the one in the story
                          The one who has fallen in love
                          I want to be the one I imagine
                          Who makes love under the sun.

I don't mind being the one who gets hurt
Or even the one who will lose
I don't even care if the ending is sad
As long as it still could be me.

I don't want to dream about who it could be
When I read about love and romance
I want to think that it could still be me
Instead of somebody else.

I want to be the one in the story
The one who has fallen in love
I want to be the one I imagine
Who makes love under the sun.

The Lights begin to fade as ——

   Vera leaves the stage during the musical outro

For a brief moment a light on Daniel on the pillowcase — then Black-out

ACT II

The setting is now a plateau overlooking the sea in Donegal. Just before dawn. A few rocks, an old upturned rowing boat

Fergal enters

The Lights come up. The Banshee wails

Fergal (*shouting out to the sky*) Leave me alone.

The wail continues

    Leave me alone. Leave me alone!

Banshee stops wailing

   Anna and Vera enter

Anna (*seeing Fergal and creeping up behind him*) Boo.
Fergal Oh God! What brought the two of you out here?
Anna Your idea. Remember? The dawn coming up and all that.
Fergal Magical, isn't it?
Vera It's freezing.
Fergal Ack no. After a while you'll lose yourself and not think about the cold when you have the like of this before you. I come here because it brings out the best in me. I think it's good for the soul, you know: the peace; the silence; the stillness.
Anna It is very peaceful.
Fergal Listen to the silence. Let's just sit here and say nothing for a while — try it — come on. I want absolute silence. Not a word. Dream and wish to your heart's content and somehow you think just for one night those wishes could possibly come true.

They are silent

Vera (*to herself*) I wish Dessie was here, the bastard.

The Banshee wails

    What's that?

Anna It's the wind.

Vera It sounds like somebody howling.

Fergal It's the Banshee.

Vera (*getting up; animated and excited*) Listen, listen. Do you hear her? Do you hear her?

Anna (*frightened*) It's the wind; it's just the wind. Isn't it, Fergal?

Vera Yes, I think I know why you are wailing.

Fergal She is wailing to warn somebody there is going to be a death.

Anna Oh God. Don't be saying things like that.

Vera I am listening to you, Banshee. You are wailing because they wrote you off just because you got old and they couldn't hack it. Maybe she was going through the change.

Fergal Be careful of the Banshee.

Vera She could have been just like us.

Anna Fergal, take us back to the hotel.

Vera Yes. Just like us. Just got old. You were not born a banshee. They made you a banshee.

Fergal People around here fear the Banshee.

Vera And the wailing is her revenge.

Song No. 4: Land of Magic and Wonder

Fergal (*singing*) In this land of magic and wonder
Where fairies and goblins and little elves roam
Out there somewhere a terrible wailing
Way beyond the sea and the foam.

Vera It's the Banshee, sayin' listen to me
It's the Banshee, callin' out to the sky
The poor Banshee was like you and me
She just didn't want to lie down and die.

Fergal In this land of magic and wonder
Out there lives a wailing old slag
Her torturous screams can be heard in the stillness
They call her the mad and withered old hag.

Vera It's the Banshee, sayin' listen to me
It's the Banshee, callin' out to the sky
The poor Banshee was like you and me
She just didn't want to lie down and die.

Fergal   In this land of magic and wonder
                        Where fairies and goblins and little elves roam
                        Out there somewhere a terrible wailing
                        Way beyond the sea and the foam.

The Banshee wails

Vera Fergal, you said here, tonight, you can dream and wish and anything
can happen.
Fergal Yes but the Banshee should not be tampered with.
Vera But isn't this the land of magic and wonder and anything can happen
tonight? Yes, tonight I could get my wish, Anna — to have my say.

She screams out to the Banshee

Fergal All right, all right. But you have to be quiet. Silent wishes. Close your
eyes.

They close their eyes and wish

Fergal exits

The two are left alone. They stand with their eyes closed

Vera This is daft. The whole point of my wish is to say it out loud so she can
hear.
Anna Vera, all this Banshee stuff is putting the fear of God into me.
Vera She is on our side; remember she was once a woman like you and me.
Anna Oh, God, I wish I was back in Belfast. (*She opens her eyes*)

Fergal reappears as Dessie in a trendy denim jacket

Jesus Christ. Look. It's Dessie. It's your Dessie.
Vera Oh my God. That's what I was wishing.
Dessie All right, Vera. Long time no see. All right Anna.
Vera (*tentatively*) You are looking well Dessie. See you've lost a bit of
weight.
Dessie Aye. Susie has me on a fruit diet. Desperate case.
Vera Susie buy your clothes too?
Dessie Aye. She likes me to look trendy.
Vera Does Susie remember your angina tablet every morning?
Dessie Now now, no nippy sweeties, Vera. Susie likes you.

Vera Why? Why does Susie like me? I have never had a conversation with Susie apart from handing her her change in the shop and saying thanks — so why would Susie like me?

Dessie Well, she thinks you have worn well.

Vera Oh she likes me because I am a maintenance expert and that is enough for Susie.

Dessie She is very fussy, not everybody Susie likes.

Vera Nice of Susie to like me. I wonder would Susie be so generous if I was competition for her, but Susie knows that Vera isn't because Susie knows that Dessie's not interested in anybody that might make him feel that he is fifty years of age.

Dessie Vera, why are you so bitter? That wee girl has done nothing on you.

Vera Dessie. When you left me did you or did you not hump practically half of our road and were making your way down the other half when you got fed up and married somebody twenty-five years younger?

Dessie Aye, why have you got a problem with that?

Vera No, but if I had done that what would you have thought?

Dessie You wouldn't do that.

Vera If I had.

Dessie Nothing to do with me.

Vera Liar. You would have said whore. Whore. Vera is a whore and now look at her, she has married a man of twenty and I would have been the talk of the district — right?

Dessie Maybe.

Vera Would you marry somebody twenty-five years older than yourself?

Dessie What — that would make her seventy-five — Vera — get a grip will you, for Christ sake get real. What man wouldn't want a woman twenty-five years younger who loves them, respects them, looks up to them, makes them feel young again, in love again? She thinks I am wonderful, I think she is wonderful, we are in love — what did you want me to say to all that? — Oh no I couldn't take all that because it won't happen to my Vera and that's not fair — for God sake try and be a wee bit generous will you? Try and be happy for people who have what you want instead of begrudging it because you can't have it yourself or you are going to end up a very unhappy old woman.

Vera You want me to pretend to be happy so it doesn't disturb you. And yes I do begrudge you your happiness, because you don't deserve it. Now you can go.

Dessie (*muttering under his breath*) You are one sad bitch. (*About to leave, then turning back*) At least she is a proper wife.

Vera Oh you mean she slaves after you.

Dessie No I mean she is actually home sometimes. Like she doesn't use the house like a friggin' B&B.

Vera Think I was going to stay home every night and luk at your gub.
Dessie Then why the hell did you ever get married?
Vera Stupidity.
Dessie Aye, same here.
Vera You never wanted a wife. You wanted a cook. You wanted a cleaner.
Dessie A cook, a cleaner, for God sake, all I ever got for my tea was notes
saying "Make your own".
Vera You're lucky you got a note.
Dessie Self, self, self, Vera. The only person you ever thought about.
Vera Yes, because Vera was the only person that ever cared about Vera.
Dessie Give my head peace. You haven't changed. Motor mouth. Somebody
should clamp your jaws and give your face a break.

He goes to exit

Vera Cissy prick.
Dessie Not any more Vera, not any more.

Dessie exits

Vera Didn't I tell you he was a gobshite? Didn't I? Look at him. Fruit diet
— and Barbie dressing him, it's pathetic. Susie likes me. Did you ever…
(*She lights a cigarette*)
Anna He had a point, Vera.
Vera Oh aye, like what?
Anna You can't expect people not to go looking for happiness just because
you don't approve of what is making them happy. Oh Jesus, Vera. What's
happening? Was Dessie really here?
Vera I don't know. I don't know what's happening.

Fergal enters

Fergal, what's happening here?

Fergal takes the cigarette from her — he makes the lit cigarette disappear

Fergal That was a brilliant trick.
Vera That wasn't a trick — (*realizing*) that was magic.

The Banshee wails

I want Susie here. The Banshee wants Susie here. We want her to know
what it's like to see your husband run off with a bimbo.

Anna Stop it, we shouldn't be interfering with all this.
Fergal All right, Vera. Anything can happen tonight until the dawn comes.
Vera Good.

Fergal exits

Anna I want a wish — I wish you would stop all this, Vera.
Vera Anna, for Christ sake this is for you, for us, for all of us, before we disappear into the wrinkles box forever.

Fergal enters as Susie

Anna (*noticing Susie*) Oh Jesus Christ.
Susie Vera, you wanted to see me.
Vera Susie — Susie, what did you see in him?
Susie What?
Vera You know, the man you are married to. What do you see in him?
Susie I love Dessie.
Vera I know, but why?
Susie I love him and he loves me and that's enough. So leave me alone. He looks after me, he cares about me, he respects me. He ——
Vera He won't go off with a younger woman.
Susie Yes — yes — so what is wrong with that? — I watched my Da do that to my mother — I watched him looking at them when he was with her, eyeing up my friends when I brought them to the house and it made me sick, just sick — then he left, he left her for somebody fifteen years younger and it nearly killed her. She wouldn't go out of the house after that. She just disappeared into herself — became invisible — the bastard made her feel like she'd wasted her life — he took away her confidence — he made her feel ugly and she was so lovely — I swore no man would do that to me. I will always be the younger woman to Dessie. Always.
Vera Banshee, is there any hope? Is there any hope? Susie. Just go.

As Susie exits she turns to Vera

Susie If you had loved him you wouldn't have lost him. He needed to be loved. To be told he was a man again.

Susie exits

Anna You know it's true.

The Banshee starts to wail

Vera Am I going crazy? Are we the only two people who think this is wrong?
Anna If you want to hang on to a man, you've got to work at it.

Fergal enters

Fergal My turn, Vera McClure. Well now I had a mate who had a terrible
time with the weemin, all around him his mates were dating this one and
that but God help him, Francie had nothing going for him. Ginger hair;
beaky nose but he never let it rest. He was determined — men don't have
it as easy as you think — I wrote a song about it.
Vera I suppose you're going to sing it for us.
Fergal I think I could be persuaded.

Song No. 5: Francie McMahon

(Singing)   Francie McMahon was a devil for the crack
                     The life and soul from here to Gueedore
                     He played the fiddle he sang and he danced
                     But inside his heart was sore.
                     But Francie hid it and never let on
                     And was as cocky and happy seemin'
                     What Francie hid was hurtin' deep down
                     He had a terrible time meetin' weemin.

                     What Francie hid was hurtin' deep down
                     So he took himself off to New York

                     Then one brute of a day lo and behold
                     We had to check if our eyes was deceiving
                     Down the main street drove Francie McMahon
                     In a car that was not for believing
                     Francie was dressed like an oil tycoon
                     In an open top sports cabriolet
                     The rain was pourin' and the wind was cuttin'
                     As Francie shouted "Have a nice day".

                     The rain was pourin' and the wind was cuttin'
                     As Francie shouted "Have a nice day".

                     Now Francie was hardly to be seen in the pub
                     He'd be cruising with the girls on show
                     They fought over him like he was cock of the hoop
                     To sail round like the Marys of Dungloe

They oohed and aahed over the plush leather seats
He could choose what girl tuk his fancy
They blasted the stereo, reclined the seats
But none of them ever saw Francie.

They blasted the stereo, reclined the seats
But none of them ever saw Francie.

Then one fateful night on a hairpin bend
As Francie was headin' for the dance
He didn't see the flock of stray sheep
And was found lying deep in a trance.
When Francie woke up in ward seventeen
His heap of scrap had been towed away
A lovely young nurse said "Don't worry now
Sure what's an oul cabriolet?"

A lovely young nurse said "Don't worry now
Sure what's an oul cabriolet?

As the weeks went on Francie grew strong
The nurse and him became friends
They laughed and talked and joked and got on
'Til Francie was on the mend
The day he left they were both in love
And he knew it wasn't just a fancy
She didn't need his sports cabriolet
She saw right to the soul of Francie.

She didn't need his sports cabriolet
She saw right to the soul of Francie.

She didn't need his sports cabriolet
She saw right to the soul of Francie.

Vera (*to Fergal*) She was his friend first. I like that. Is this true?
Fergal Well — do you want it be?
Anna Yes — yes I do.
Fergal Then it is.
Vera Wishful thinking if it happened the other way round.
Fergal Exactly what this night is about. Realizing your dreams.
Vera Then I wish men could see into the souls of women like women can
see into theirs. If Francie McMahon had been a woman the only thing she

would have walked out of that hospital with would have been a bunch of grapes. Do you think a lovely young male nurse could see past an ugly woman to her soul? I mean could you?

Fergal can't answer

That's what I've always wanted. To be loved for myself. I tried to be myself with Dessie but it just drove him away. At parties I could be just as funny, just as opinionated and he hated it. He'd call me into a corner and say, "Vera. See you? You are letting me down. You are showing me up. You would be all right if you kept your motor mouth shut." So what is the point in trying to be equal, you can't win. Am I right, Fergal?

Fergal Yeah. You're righ

Vera So to hell with them: if I can't find love, I'll just go for sex — there will always be somebody looking a quickie and I'll even keep my motor mouth shut.

Anna You should hear yourself sometimes.

Vera I do, I'm not deaf.

Anna Gettin' on like that.

Vera Like what.

Anna Like you were some sort of nymphomaniac.

Vera Maybe I am, so what.

Anna I don't believe you need men that bad.

Vera Saves on the batteries doesn't it.

Fergal turns away in embarrasment. During the following he drapes a scarf around his shoulders to play the character of Stella

Anna No wonder people call you a whore.

Vera Who calls me a whore?

Anna People.

Vera What people?

Anna Lots of people.

Vera Who?

Anna Nearly everybody calls you a whore.

Vera Give me names.

Anna I will not.

Vera It's you, isn't it, it's you that calls me a whore.

Anna Me — it's not me — I stand up for you, it's everybody else.

Vera Who calls me a whore?

Anna I stick up for you. It's me who defends you.

Vera Who calls me a whore?

Fergal turns around as Stella

Stella from the fancy goods. So you call me a whore.

Stella Last year's staff Christmas dinner you couldn't take your eyes off my husband.

Vera Fuck's sake. I only asked him to pass me the carrots to save me stretchin' over him and I thought b'Jesus you were going to need a heart ambulance.

Stella And later you nearly had your breasts in his face.

Vera What is he, a midget?

Stella He was sitting down at the time.

Vera Well I want to talk to you, Stella. So you sit down.

Stella Oh no. I don't want to hear this.

Vera Well I'm afraid you're just going to have to.

Stella I knew it, I knew it. I knew the bastard had another woman.

Vera Take it easy love — I don't know if he has or he hasn't. That's got nothing to do with me.

Stella Oh God, Vera. My heart near stopped. I just thought — oh God — it's just when somebody tells you to sit down, you think the worst. And I keep waiting for the phone call to tell me he has been seen with her or the letter he leaves in his trouser pocket, or lipstick under the seat in the car, or the blonde hair in his comb or somebody saying "Sit down, Stella" just like you've said. Oh God, I'm sorry. My head is away with it all. It's just when you get to our age and your men's eyes wander it's desperate.

Vera Then why do you despise me, Stella?

Stella It's not just you.

Anna Who is it?

Stella Everybody. Anybody that might take him away from me. Anybody better than me.

Anna Has he ever had an affair?

Stella No. He says he never would.

Anna Does he tell you he loves you, buy you flowers, remember your birthday?

Stella All those things.

Vera Well then for Christ sake get a grip.

Stella You see Vera it's not you — it's me. You know since the change and everything you start to feel like you have lost your grip.

Anna Stella. You don't know how lucky you are.

Stella What.

Anna Go and tell your Peter he's a decent man.

Stella What? How do you know my Peter is decent? What do you know about my Peter? Have you talked to him or what? Is it you who phones our house and doesn't leave a message? Is it!!!

Vera Stella, love, you are in a bad way.

Stella Sorry — sorry — I am going crazy — you see my Peter was so romantic, used to write me love poems — you know the type — "You are like the first blush of spring" — "Your skin is as fair as the snow, your eyes glisten like the dew on the grass" and I loved it. That was the way he expressed himself and I felt on top of the world. I look at these poems now Vera and I cry because I am not like that any more, I mean if he loved me because I was like that then, how could he love me now? It's not fair — nature is always beautiful — like every year there is the first blush of spring and the snow is always white and the dew is there every morning and it's sad, so it is. Because it doesn't get old like us. Nobody ever writes "I will love you when you turn to slush, or when your petals wither up and drop off". It's not fair. Like you can't live up to nature anymore.

Fergal exits

Anna I use to read all them love poems. "How do I love thee? Shall I count the ways?" They made me cry. I wanted somebody to write those things to me.

Vera Like Stella's Peter?

Fergal enters as Peter

Peter Hello girls.

Vera Peter!

Peter (*admiring the view*) This is beautiful. This is really beautiful.

> I would that we were, my beloved,
> White birds on the foam of the sea!
> We tire of the flame of the meteor,
> Before it can fade and flee.
> And the flame of the blue star of twilight,
> Hung low on the rim of the sky,
> Has awakened in our hearts, my beloved,
> A sadness that may not die — Yeats.

Vera Gimme a break.

Anna How's your wife, Peter?

Peter The woman is going to drive herself into an institution.

Vera You have made her a very unhappy woman because of that oul romantic shite in the first place.

Peter What she wanted. She demanded, "Write to me, Peter. Be romantic, write me a poem, Peter." Before I met her I hardly knew what a poem was.

Anna Oh, so it's all her fault, Peter?

Peter No it's my fault. I wanted to be the man in the Milk Tray ad. I wanted

to make it special. I wanted to make it like it was in the films. So, yeah —
it was probably my fault.

Vera Is there another woman, Peter?

Peter She's made me an addict; an incurable romantic.

Vera And what have you done to her?

Peter Well, if I wasn't having affairs she would think I was. Nothing would
stop her thinking that. So I thought to myself, what harm in doing what I
am going to get accused of anyway? Stella, Stella, Stella — it was endless
bouquets. It's flowers for the anniversary of our first kiss, the first row,
flowers for the anniversary of the day we made up after the first row, the
anniversary for when the kids were conceived, the anniversary —

Vera Then leave her and give her peace.

Peter She would go to pieces, I know that. Look I am no martyr staying with
a woman that drives me crazy. You all drive me crazy. But, better the crazy
you know than the crazy you don't. I am in love with being in love, I love
it — love it — but what do you do? I am a loveaholic — desperate — it's
a curse — have to go.

*Peter magically produces two roses; he hands one to Anna, which she takes.
He goes to hand one to Vera but realizes it's a bad idea*

I'm meeting a friend. Just a friend.

Fergal exits

Anna No-one's ever given me a flower before, can you imagine, the
anniversary of your first kiss, the anniversary of your first row?

Vera snaps the rose away from Anna and throws it down

Vera Jesus Christ. You're a stupid cow. Don't encourage men like that.
Think of the misery he's causing, the lives he's wrecking. Prats like that
should have a Government health warning pinned to them.

Fergal enters, and picks up the rose

Fergal Now now. Don't start condemning poetry, Vera. It's one of the finest
things that men can do; one of the greatest gifts that one human being can
give to another.

He flirtatiously hands Vera the rose

Vera You just give it a rest.

He sits down and occasionally looks at Vera as he recites his poem

Fergal   When she rises in her crimson glory
                     My love in all her splendour
                     She fills my empty heart with love
                     And my soul with deepest pleasure.
                     My love is like the rising sun
                     In her beauty and her wonder
                     Slowly and brilliantly she rises
                     Her fair skin glows as it does yonder.

Fergal hands Vera the rose, she takes it — confused

Anna Did you write that for somebody?
Fergal Maybe.
Vera Who?
Fergal The woman I will love someday.
Anna What if she doesn't look like that.
Fergal Like what?
Anna Crimson and glowin' and fair and beautiful.
Fergal (*jokingly poetic*) Then I will search until I find what I am looking for.
Vera (*throwing the rose down*) You see? You are just like all the rest.
Fergal What do you mean, normal?
Anna Yes I think it is absolutely normal.
Vera Jesus are you saying, you can't be loved if you're not beautiful.

Fergal lifts the rose

Anna No, it's just what most men look for and who can blame them.
Vera Then why do you bother gettin' out of bed in the morning — why don't
  you just lie there with the duvet over your face?
Anna What?
Vera When you get up in the morning and look in the mirror do you not say
  to yourself, "Ah Jesus Christ I am a barker. There's no point in me getting
  up. Nobody's ever gonna love me again?" Why don't you just sign yourself
  into an ugly camp? Yes. That's what we should do, set up ugly camps and
  as soon as we become offensive to the human eye it's off you go — and you
  won't be able to hide. You won't be able to protest because you'll get
  reported: Hello an ugly woman has been seen in Royal Avenue, and they'll
  come for you in wee vans, like dogcatchers.

The Banshee wails

Fergal There were these two fairies, a man and a woman, and they were in love — they swore undying love to each other —well, one day the male fairy announces that he is going to the land of Eternal Youth, Tir Na Nog and the female fairy said, "Will you still love me when I get old and you are not?" "Certainly I will," said the male fairy. "I will always love you." So anyway he goes off to the land of Eternal Youth and he comes back and the female fairy is old and withered and he says, "I still love you. I love your soul. I love your spirit." "Then why can't you look at me?" says the female fairy. And he can't because she has become so withered — "Look at me," she screams — and he can't. "I can't look at you," he says, "but I still love you." "No you don't", she screams, "you can't look at my body," and the male fairy says "You have to accept that you get old," and she screams and screams until he can no longer bear to listen. So she banishes him into the hills calling him a Pooka, a bad fairy and she is still screamin' to this very day — and that is the real story of how the Banshee became the Banshee; she just would not accept she was no longer beautiful so when we hear her screaming it's because she knows that the Pooka is somewhere around.

Vera I know what this night is all about; it's to shut me up, isn't it? To stop me being angry, an angry bitter oul cow, just like her, make me put up and shut up.

Anna For God sake Vera, shut up. I am so sick of all this, so bloody sick of it — I am up to here with it — I am away back home because you and your life and what you can't get is bloody boring, boring. I came away here to get away from everything, to see Daniel, to lose myself.

Vera Why do you always have to lose yourself? It's because you live in all that stupid oul romantic rubbish in your head. Why don't you just wise up? Why don't you face up to your miserable life and do something about it?

Song No. 6: Don't Shatter My Dreams

Anna (*singing*)   Alone my dreams and me
Away from this loveless world
My comfort, my warmth
My escape from the cold.

Leave me as I am
Let me sail and let me fly
Let me glide on clouds
Don't bring me down from the sky.

Don't shatter my dreams, handle with care.
They keep me safe from the stale grey air.
Don't shatter my dreams, handle with care.
They keep me safe from the stale grey air.

Don't shatter my dreams, handle with care.
They keep me safe from the stale grey air.
Don't shatter my dreams, handle with care.
They keep me safe from the stale grey air.

Instrumental, one verse

Don't shatter my dreams, handle with care.
They keep me safe from the stale grey air.
Don't shatter my dreams, handle with care.
They keep me safe from the stale grey air.

I believe people can love each other for reasons other than sex or beauty. People just want to wake up beside people in the morning and know that they are the special person for them, it doesn't matter what the rest of the world thinks about them. They are together, they have each other and they want to be together for ever. They are happy to grow old together and love and cherish each other until death do them part.

Vera So your husband really loves you? He's just too embarrassed to say?

Anna Yes, he does; in his own way, he does.

Vera Then bring him here and ask him.

Anna NO — no, I know him. I am all right as I am.

Vera I'm going to bring him here. I'm going to ask your Marty if he loves you, if he cherishes you. The dawn is nearly up, Anna. there's not much time left.

Anna I said no, Vera.

Vera (*defiantly to Fergal*) Marty.

Fergal becomes Marty

Marty This man goes to Lourdes and he gets off the plane and he sees all these zimmers and crutches and wheelchairs and ambulances all empty and he gets all excited and he says, "My God have all these people been cured?" Just as he is about to drop to his knees and thank the Lord, he sees a big sign saying — "Daniel O'Donnell playing tonight — car park full…"

Vera Hello, Marty.

Marty What about yis girls, where's your broomsticks?

Anna Marty, don't you love me?

Marty Love, love. I've been there twenty-five years, haven't I? The train robbers didn't get that long.

Vera Ask him why he never makes love to you.

Anna Marty, why do you never make love to me?

Marty Was your woman drinking or something, Vera? Hey, wait 'til you hear this one. This couple in this multi-storey flat are making love. So the

first night she says to him, "Who do you think about when you are making
love to me?" and he says, "Michelle Pfeiffer", and his wife got dead
excited, you know, being compared to Michelle Pfeiffer. So the sex was
brilliant. Next night she says the same thing and he says, "Pamela
Anderson" and the sex was brilliant. So the next night he thinks he should
ask her. So they are humpin' away and he says, whose body would you like
me to be and she whispers something in his ear. Next thing he jumps up,
straight out the window, down twenty storeys, and splat on to the pavement
— dead — so she is hanging over the body crying, "I said do you fancy a
Mcdonald's, not Daniel O'Donnell's".

Anna Why do you despise him so much?

Marty Who?

Anna Daniel.

Marty 'Cos he is a buck eejit.

Anna You can't think any deeper than that about anybody, can you?

Marty He's a big girl's armpit.

Anna Does it not occur to you when you say that, that it might hurt me?

Marty Sure what is it to you?

Anna My life line.

Marty Christ sake, wise up. Did you ever — life line — aye right enough,
he luks like a big drip — get it — drip.

Anna Let me ask you something — did you ever think when you stopped
wanting to make love to me what it did to me?

Marty That's enough…

Anna Can you not take me seriously because I am no longer sexy?

Marty Shut up.

Anna I want you to talk to me, Marty — as a woman, as a lover, as a friend.

Marty Wise up.

Anna Talk to me, Marty.

Marty Why? I was never good at that — I work hard, don't I? I've never
lifted my hand to you, yet — what do you want me to do, sing to you?

Anna I want to be loved, to be made love to, to talk, to feel good about myself.

Marty I'm not interested in that.

Anna Why?

Marty I don't know.

Anna Why?

Marty Just — just — I don't know. How am I supposed to know?

Anna My body is no longer attractive.

Marty Maybe.

Anna Do you think yours is?

Marty I don't think about it.

Anna Are you a homosexual?

Marty What the hell are you on about?

Anna Why then do you have no interest in sex?

Marty Calling me a queer? Calling me a queer! Just 'cos I don't do it with you.

Anna Then is there someone else.

Marty NO.

Anna Then why? Why?

Marty I do think about sex, I think about sex, all the time — calling me a queer.

Anna That got you going Marty — what am I supposed to think when you turn away from me every night?

Marty I have — I have my books — all right — I have my books — I love sex.

Anna What?

Marty All kinds of sex if you want to know.

Anna Dirty books.

Marty They are not dirty ——

Anna You — porn magazines.

Marty All men do.

Anna And you fantasize, is it you in the fantasy, is it you screwing those women in the pictures?

Marty Anna, for Jesus sake, this is enough.

Anna Answer me.

Marty (*to Vera*) Did you put her up to this?

Anna Answer me.

Marty No — I don't know — I — look for God sake Anna.

Anna The truth, that's all I want — is it you?

Marty Yes — yes, of course it is.

Anna When I read my books it is always someone else, someone else. You even took away my fantasy that I could be loved again that I could have somebody who will see me, love me and listen to me and why? Because you have made me invisible. That is all I have to say — and when you make fun of Daniel O'Donnell and all us silly women, does it not occur to you that he recognizes that we can still love, still feel, still dream? All those things that you never wanted to know about me.

Marty Anna, what the frig are you talking about?

Anna Vera, tell him to go.

Vera indicates with a nod that Marty should clear off

Marty I hope youse find your broomsticks, girls.

Fergal exits

Anna What now? What do I do now? Now that I know — I was all right, we could have gone on like that forever — I was OK.

Vera You weren't OK.

Anna So — at least I kept him, he was there, what if he goes, what if he just says fuck it and goes? Where will I go? Who will want to know me? What do you say when your man leaves you? He left me because he didn't love me? No, Vera I would rather live with him knowing he doesn't love me than have to live on my own and everybody else knowing he didn't love me. Don't you say anything — Vera. I wish I was like you — you're brave.

Fergal enters

Vera Bravery had nothing to do with me splitting up with Dessie. It was survival Anna. Survival of my sanity. You see I liked myself, Anna — I respected myself. Come on, Anna, the sex Marty has going on in his head can never be compared to a real person. It's fifteen year old girls slithering about in baby oil.

Anna How am I supposed to compete with that?

Vera You can't. Every time he turns on the telly there's another gorgeous girl with her mouth wrapped round a bar of chocolate.

Anna Sex must be everything if they even use it to sell chocolate.

Vera Yeah. We couldn't sell a bag of coal.

Anna Tits. The perter the better.

Vera Bums. The tighter the better ... And penises.

Anna I don't suppose it really matters what size they are.

Fergal See — what can you do? It's basic, it's normal, it's natural.

Anna (*resigned*) It's just natural, as Fergal says.

Fergal Vera. You may not like it but look out there. Look at nature. Will you or anybody ever stop that tide coming in, going out, the dawn rising, the sun setting or men desiring beautiful things? That's been happening since the world began. We have no control over it, none — it's nature. It is natural for us to want beautiful things. We just can't help it. Am I right, Vera?

Vera My granny had ten children and it nearly killed her. She was pregnant for the most of her life because it was natural. She died having the eleventh but what could she do? It was nature. Could you have stood and watched her bleed to death and accept that that was nature? As natural as the tide comin' in and out, as the sun setting? As the dawn rising? As natural as men desiring beautiful things? Could you? Could you? You see somebody didn't. Somebody had the imagination to see how awful it was, somebody said to themselves, nature is destroying these women and we have to stop nature being cruel.

Fergal kisses Vera

Fergal   When she rises in her crimson glory
                    My love in all her splendour
                    She fills my empty heart with love
                    And my soul with deepest pleasure.

Vera Wish somebody would write something like that for me.

Fergal It is for you ,Vera.

Vera What?

Fergal I want that to be for you.

Vera Now come on Fergal, you know I am nothing like what you described
in your poems.

Fergal You are to me. I am talking about inner beauty — the crimson glow
of the soul, the rising sun is the spirit that fills me with pleasure.

Vera Fergal. What are you saying?

Fergal Well, why not? We know a lot about each other after the night — I
have seen into your soul, Vera — I could love you.

Vera Are you serious?

Fergal Isn't it what you want?

Vera hesitates. He puts his arms out. She goes to him and kisses him

There is a puff of smoke and Fergal disappears

Anna (*screaming*) I'm so angry.

The Banshee wails followed by flute music

The Lights fade up indicating the dawn

Anna and Vera turn to watch it

Song No. 7: Finale Song

(*Singing*)   We won't go easy we'll go down protestin'
                     The rest of our life is too long for restin'
                     All we're asking is the right to reply
                     When we're told our passion must lie down and die.

                     We're women on the verge
                     And we won't take ignorin'
                     No sex hospice for us
                     We're still up for scoring

So come on sisters
Don't let them win
We may be over forty
But we can still sin, sin, sin, sin.

We won't go easy; we'll go down protestin'
The rest of our life is too long for restin'
All we're askin' is the right to reply
When we're told our passion must lie down and die.

Lights fade to black-out

FURNITURE AND PROPERTY LIST

ACT I

On stage:　Two single beds with bedding. *On* **Anna***'s*: bag containing Daniel
O'Donnell pillowcase, soap bag containing tub of Nivea Creme,
purse containing money. *On* **Vera***'s*: large toilet bag containing tub
of expensive night cream, make-up remover, cotton wool; towel
Two bedside cabinets. *On* **Anna***'s*: pair of spectacles, huge romantic
novel
Dressing-table
Vera's suit case. *In it*: make-up bag, bottle of vodka
Telephone

Off stage:　Dressing-gown and nightdress (**Vera**)
Tray. *On it*: two glasses of vodka and two opened bottles of lemonade
(**Fergal**)
Packet of cigarettes and lighter (**Vera**)
Two more glasses of vodka (**Fergal**)
Two unopened bottles of lemonade (**Fergal**)
Dressing gown (**Anna**)

Personal:　**Fergal**: bottle opener

ACT II

On stage:　Rocks
Old upturned rowing boat

Personal:　**Vera**: packet of cigarettes and lighter
Fergal (as **Peter**): two roses

LIGHTING PLOT

Property fittings required: nil
Interior: Hotel room. Exterior: Plateau overlooking the sea in Donegal

ACT I

To open: Bring up overall general lighting

Cue 1   **Vera**: (*singing*) "Who makes love under the sun."   (Page 20)
          Lights begin to fade

Cue 2   **Vera** exits   (Page 20)
          Bring up light on Daniel O'Donnell pillowcase. Black-out

ACT II

Cue 3   **Fergal** enters   (Page 21)
          Bring up overall general lighting "Before dawn"

Cue 4   **Vera** kisses **Fergal**   (Page 39)
          Black-out

Cue 5   Banshee wails followed by flute music   (Page 39)
          Bring up dawn effect

Cue 6   **Anna** and **Vera**: (*singing*) "… must lie down and die."   (Page 40)
          Fade to black-out

EFFECTS PLOT

ACT I

ACT II

Cue 13   **Vera** kisses **Fergal**   (Page 39)
             Puff of smoke

Cue 14   **Anna**: "I'm so angry."   (Page 39)
             The Banshee wails; flute music; fade when ready

1. I Won't Go Easy

Vera - Anna

Cue: **Vera** That's what I'm scared of. Panic buying.

acc. Colla Voce

2. Donegal

Fergal

Cue: **Fergal** I'm going to sing for you.

1,5. I—— dream of the dawn in the
2. On—— still sum - mer nights my——
3. This—— fo - reign land can -
4. Should— I—————— die on this

land of my birth my—— soul hears its si - lent call———— to the
heart— is torn as I stand on this fo - reign shore——— Oh——
not— e - rase those—— pic - tures so clear in my mind——— where the
a - li - en shore I—— pray that my soul will a - way——— a -

ma - gic and glo - ry of that won - der - ous sight of the dawn o - ver
Do - ne - gal at each—— ris - ing dawn I will yearn for you
set - ting sun—— brings—— peace to my soul oh my dear land I've
cross— the seas—— to my hea - ven on earth Do - ne - gal, where my

Do - ne - gal.———
ev - er more.———
left— be - hind.———
spi - rit will stay.———

Please note.
Instrumental verse after verse 2.

3. I Want To Be

Vera

Cue: **Vera** ...you are the one that needs help.

1,4. I want to be the one in the sto-ry the
2. I don't-mind be-ing the one who gets hurt or

one who has fal-len in love I want to be the one I i-ma-gine who
e-ven the one who will lose I don't e-ven care if the end-ing is sad as

makes love un-der the sun. me. 3. I don't want to dream a-bout
long as it still could be

who it could be when I read a-bout love and ro-mance

I want to think that it could still be me in-stead of some-bo-dy else.

4. Land of Magic and Wonder

Fergal - Vera

Cue: **Vera** And the wailing is her revenge.

Senza tempo (freely) in a traditional style

In this land of ma - gic and— won - der where fai-ries and gob-lins and lit-tle elves roam

out there— some-where a ter-ri-ble wail-ing way be-yond the sea— and the foam.

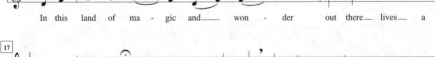

It's the Ban-shee, sayin' lis-ten to me it's the Ban-shee, callin' out to the sky the

poor— Ban-shee was like you and me she just did-n't want to lie down and die.

In this land of ma - gic and— won - der out there— lives— a

wail - ing old slag her tor-tu - rous screams can be heard in the still - ness

they— call her the mad— and with - ered old hag.

*All verses a capella or
with the option of a
low 'G' drone*

5. Francie McMahon

wee - min.____ What Fran - cie hid____ was hur - tin' deep down____ so he
day".____ The rain was pour - in' and the wind____ was cut - tin' as____
Francie.____ They blast - ed the ste - re - o, re - clined____ the seats____ but____

took him self____ off to New York. Then Fran - cie. Then
Fran - cie shout - ed "Have a nice day". Now
none of them____ e - ver saw

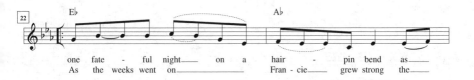

one fate - ful night____ on a hair - pin bend as____
As the weeks went on____ Fran - cie____ grew strong the____

Fran - cie____ was head - in' for the dance he did - n't____ see the____
nurse____ and____ him be - came friends they laughed____ and talked____ and____

flock of____ stray sheep and was found ly - ing deep in a trance. When
joked and____ got on til____ Fran - cie was on the____ mend The

Fran - cie____ woke____ up in ward se - ven - teen his____ heap of scrap had been____ towed a -
day he____ left____ they were both____ in love and he knew it____ was - n't just a

way— A love-ly— young nurse— said "Don't wor - ry now sure—
fan-cy— she did - n't need— his— sports cab - rio - let she saw

Repeat last time only: Rit towards end.

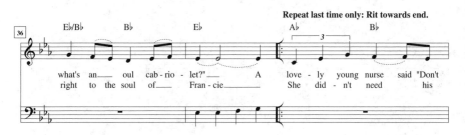

what's an— oul cab - rio - let?"— A love - ly young nurse said "Don't
right to the soul of— Fran - cie— She did - n't need his

(last x only)

wor - ry now— sure what's an— oul cab - rio - let?"
sports cabrio - let she saw right to the soul of— Fran - cie.

6. Don't Shatter My Dreams

Anna

Cue: **Vera** ...do something about it?

7. Finale Song

Vera - Anna

Cue: *The lights fade up indicating the dawn*

We— won't go ea-sy;— we'll go down pro-test-in'— the rest of our life is too long for rest-in' all we're ask-in' is the right to re-ply when we're told our pas-sion must lie down and die. We're wo-men on the verge and we won't take ig-norin' no— sex— hos-pice for us we're still up for scor-ing so come— on— sis-ters— don't— let them win we may be o-ver for-ty but we can still sin, sin, sin sin.